Memento Mori

dead leaves
fertilize trees

Cayce Burch

Contents:

Introduction

There is no more common element in all our lives than "living and dying", but the various questions surrounding life and death are often unanswerable. We can image black holes, we can build flying cars, but the most common items elude us. Early on and continuing, I encountered death in any number of circumstances, and sometimes, it wasn't so literal. I started journaling when I was 14 years old, and over time, journaling turned into poetry. Quite a few of the following selected works are the result of seeking to let go and heal from my experiences. This is my first published book after writing for 17 years.

Memento Mori is a reminder that we are mortal and that we, along with our creations, are not permanent. It encourages us to resolve items that are 'not resolvable', to be thankful for the present, to have some perspective, and to remember to be humble. Memento Mori is a Latin phrase, but cultures around the world have some similar views on human impermanence. The subtitle, "dead leaves fertilize trees," highlights that while death is loss, recovering from loss is growth, and while we may not have all the answers, the direction before us is internal. By what we lose, we can gain more than we ever thought possible - when the shroud of grief lifts. Sometimes we have to wait, sometimes we have to push through, and sometimes we are pushed onwards by the seasonality of spring.

I've learned over time that there are at least three different forms of death: actual death, character death, and ego death. Actual death is rather final and finite, if not imbued with ideas of "thereafter". Character death happens when someone is living but has undergone such a stark negative change that they are no longer the same person. They may be consumed with addiction, self hatred, greed, mental illness, etc. Ego death is the loss of the separate sense of self, and may be caused in different ways. It may be a seemingly permanent change, it may be fleetingly temporary. Sometimes, death is metaphysical.

"Remember to Die" as the title and subject of this book is meant to illuminate, not just human impermanence, but what it means 'to live'. Humans have long struggled, not just with how to live, but with living itself; pain and struggles can make a quick exit seem like the solution. I have struggled with suicide around me and in me throughout my life. I have known quite a few people who have tried to escape pain in any number of ways, through self harm, addictions, or suicide. Since I have also struggled with these issues myself, in various ways, I try to be there for others as much as I can.

It is through these experiences that I journaled out the works laid out within this book. I'll expose another lens to view this book: "Remember to Live and Let Die". Not everything was meant to continue, and we often forget to let go 'easily'. In that vein: some works are recently written, some are not, some are general works, some are specific, and some never happened. All of the works were never meant for anyone but myself, but most of them were written so that they could be viewed by an audience. "Take what you like, and leave the rest".

My work has, first and foremost, been reminders to myself to exhume emotions and review insights found within. Most of my writing starts from a general idea and I let my subconscious mind take me on a journey where I don't know the end. I am not a writer who reviews each word and line for weeks, and I edit my work rarely. Be that as it may. Each item is built on where I was, then, and may have changed and reverted a thousand times since, but I wouldn't include anything here that I don't think has merit.

I sincerely hope that the words I wrote to myself aid you in your journey.

Cayce Burch

Acknowledgments

I want to thank my mom and dad first and foremost. No matter the trials and tribulations we have gone through, they uncovered many life mysteries and showed me the bugs underneath the rocks. Secondly, I want to thank my sisters, my stepmom, and the rest of my family. They kept me close, welcomed me in, and gave me space to vent and to heal. I could not ask for more. I want to thank my friends who lent me an ear and reminded me to laugh and relax, even in the thick of it all. I want to thank my Grandmother, who listened to me, who advised me, who encouraged me, who chided me, who showed me the blueprint before my birth, and who offered perspectives when my view was unchanging.

Lastly, I want to thank myself, for opening my ears and eyes to uncomfortable truths, for seeking out advice and information that contrasts my own, for being there for others in their struggles – despite the cost – because I learned more of myself from them, for charting the path when there seemed to be no path, for breathing slowly though it all, for continuing to breathe and wake up everyday, for cautioning myself against bitterness, for sticking to my plans, for healing, for writing, for "One day at a time", and for "Let Go and Let God".

Without everyone mentioned in the first paragraph, I could not have written the second paragraph, or any of the works within, so again, thank you.

Cayce Burch

"All stopping implies starting."
Alan Watts

Love Thyself

I've been on the road,
I've been on the tracks.
I've been on midnight flights,
I've been on redeyed bike rides.
Might've traveled here to LA – 20 times in one city, in
      one car,
So I wonder, how many miles have I traveled in my
      mind?
How many dead ends have I backtracked?
How many lanes have I crossed without looking?
How many rest stops did I actually take?
How many accidents did I narrowly avoid?
And now,
At the end of the longest rest I've ever taken,
I wonder –
How many times have I looked into the same mirror,
And not deeply loved myself
As much as I've loved another?

To Be

I look in his eyes:
A lost man walking.

I open my mouth:
"At your lowest,
you have the greatest potential".
He drones,
"They say,
'Just be you—',
but I don't *know me!*"

"They say," I say,
"be yourself,
but they miss the target.
There is no 'self' to be;
there is only:
'To Be'".

Microbes

It's easy to forget
The ancients got by with less.
No such thing as being lost;
Follow the deer trail.
No such thing as going hungry;
But that berry is poisonous.
No such thing as thirst;
It'll rain, eventually– if it doesn't, wander or dig.
No such thing as being lonely,
You are always with yourself.
No such thing as not having enough;
Trees fertilize themselves.
All of which are dependent variables,
Upon other dependent variables.
Without deer, hard to find lines of demarcation,
Without food, hard to stomach the loss,
Without water, madness runs deep,
Without the self, I couldn't see you –
Without microbes, our mind would be sterile.

My Notes

We wail,
We wail,
We wail.
Into darkness for all we've lost.

And the light responds in kind,
reminding us that the direction our feet lead
was beat before us.

Trillions of ghostly feet limp, walk, and run
this way, that way, on trail, off trail,
up trees, taking flight with wings, constructing rails.

Take comfort that everyone's lost when they started –
for: that's the only comfort you'll receive;
take comfort that they went before you, for:
the first through the door is shot.

Death, never far away, trails up behind,
interpreting signs, – cryptic to the living.
And in this journey, I trail up behind-
a narrator of a voiceless form.

My notes, cryptic as Death pointing a finger ahead,
describe the meeting of Oneself, pure and powerful.
My notes, literal as a field of food on fire,
describe how lost one would be to take a page from
            Death's book.

And these notes- were lost in a fire, a blaze seen from
            space,
And while its noise was wretched,
My lungs poured out the worst noise any demon could
            dream to hear.
I lost my voice for a week, and I wanted to scream more.

If only to see if I could wake the demons to walk the
            earth –
but only the Graces roused and walked me under the

      Mountain,
And in that deep dark, I remembered that
"All knowledge of Self is remembrance".

I remembered that
"Perception is perspective"
I remembered that
"All things, even pain, are temporary; this too shall
      end."

And in the remembrance,
A shadow was cast in the cave,
And I saw the blistering sun, burning me in seconds.
Stepping out of the light, hand out, looking at the
      ground,

I saw imprints, thousands upon thousands,
A blend of footsteps that years upon eons had worn,
A reminder that even though a body had been reduced to
      ashes,
I still had footsteps to fill and follow.

Pick Up— and Move

There's fire in the streets,
there's icewater in buildings,
there's rage in the cold heart of a mourner,
there's love in the warm heart of a rejoicer.

Contradictions contrast constantly:
a healer can injure,
an injurer can heal:
endless moments are libraries overfilled.

Can I knock on the door of the Source,
lift these wings and fly on course,
ride on the air, avoiding the tumult and minor lords –
to write as an arrow flying towards

you? Points perceived are repeated, so burn my ancient
peat, think within beat, feel without heat,
hurry patiently, impatiently do nothing. Do– then see
      what I meant.
Realize the meanings within reflections, then we shall
      meet.

Pitch your tent, build your fire,
water your garden, grow your food,
fill your mind, fill your body,
spread your garden, pick up– and move.
Pitch your tent, build your fire,
water your garden, grow your food,
fill your mind, fill your body,
spread your garden, pick up– and move.
Pitch your tent, build your fire,
water your garden, grow your food,
fill your mind, fill your body,
spread your garden, pick up–
           and move.

Complicated Simplicity

Complicate life and you will see
what is bigger than you;
simplify life, and all you will see
is you.

Neither are wholly good or bad,
neither are whole and holy or fettered and holey,
so therefore I shall break off this branch
of holly,
and offer you a couple of beautiful berries.

Perspective

Day to day, in our daily work and play
we forget that in everything we say
is a perspective, a sliver, a slice
of a world we see, either gold lace,
empty wallet, or gambling dice.
Forget how you think you are, either mean or nice,
it's how people think you are,
though only you know how you really are,
but no one really cares how you really are—
because no one truly sees how you actually are,
they see a sliver, their slice, of who they actually are,
so they mean to convey and say all this to you,
but you are just thinking of you.
How is this?
Consider this:
All I know is I.
All I know of You is how I see both I and You.
So in any Play, there is no You without an I.
If I and You becomes We,
then can We listen to see,
instead of trying to make others see what we see?

Voice Breaks

Back to the art.
All that I've thought is loaded in caravan carts.
I stomach the rage as you tell me stories,
many upon many of you– I've held my ear to the wall for
        you.

Caring is so much more than listening when you speak—
so I listen to you when your voice breaks–.
And there are so many of you. Goddamn, I'm not
        immune.
You might ask me how I'm doing, and you'll never know.

I don't think you need my headaches.
You have your own.

I see them. Dancing behind your eyes— like faded TV in
        the background.
Let's not speak of it, lets not— let us talk of what you
        find amazing,
what shows you enjoy, which person you just love to
        hate,
what vacation you love to dream, which memes you find
        funniest.

Cause lord knows we need a good laugh.
I haven't come out and shown you I really am —
because I'm not Me. I don't know how to say — I've been
        here and back.
Just as you fret over this or that— I've been there and
        back, and there again.

I keep doing as I'm doing to look after you. Maybe you'll
        look after me.
All this and that had followed— all this seen in horror,
there's only more to come. If you suffer, I'll stand with
        you–my stomach will clench
for the words you speak.

As of late, I cant stave the ragged breathing of your
          sobbing heartache,
I can't stifle your body shaking in rage, and so — I can't
          distract myself.
— My own voice brea- .

Love

Love is no band aid,
Nor a hole to fill,
Nor a need to satisfy,
Nor a feeling to cure the lonely hearted,
Nor a desperation for approval,
But the communication from deep within
To another deep within, that words could never tell.

Because we could not stop for him

Another heart ceased it's racket,
And here I am,
Barely knowing the beats that made their rhythm,
Gushing my heart for yet another loss.
Stack them up like books,
Each chapter ten thousand pages long,
Each word – worth a sun's rotation.
Names upon names,
Some not even days old,
Some grizzly and gnarled,
Some shimmering with youth,
Some burned out and gone,
Some wizened and seasoned,
Some fortunate and blessed,
Some down and out,
And all were someone's someone.

Not enough could be said
For their joys, their pains, their struggles.
They battled uphill against River Styx,
Somedays letting the river take them,
Somedays battling as if fire was in their blood.
Not enough could be said
For the love others had for them,
For the care given to them,
For the short speech: "I'd give you my kidney",
For the long speech:
"I don't have much, but let's get the fuck outta here",
For the wordless moments: "I'm here".
But here we are, mourning
Day into night, up late into the morning,
Bleary eyed for memories once had,
And now on a pedestal.

Let's honor them
By taking care of ourselves:
By enjoying the long road home,
By passing the torch and keeping it lit,

By forging ahead and laying down more road,
By marking off dead ends and cliffs,
By keeping our smiles genuine,
By holding the spark in our eyes,
By lasting until "Death kindly stops for us,
Because we could not stop for him".

Two

The wise take a path and make two:
one to advise for, to open doors,
one to warn against, so you can pay the rent,
but still you defend till you're blue,
every path you make in the woods alone.
It's all understood:
you don't need anyone cause you see the sun,
but after you looked into the suns book,
a purple dot blinds your thoughts,
losing detail in arrogance through your stance,
so others see what you project and in return inspect,
ready to prove you wrong just for fun.
Me too, though I seek and hear- old and new voices,
that lay dormant like your doormat,
silently pondering into the great unknown.
Where are the voices that counter my banter?
Let me shake your hand,
let me trace a story in the sand,
let you expose my weak defense,
let you better my stance,
because somewhere between, truth leans–
evasive but decisive and so enticing.
Most 'truth' is just perspective that has been elected
to be the 'true' road to travel by.
When coming to a fork in the road,
you can or you can't;
you will or you won't;
you keep on or you go home;
to refresh and replenish,
resolving tomorrow to break that ice.
One million thoughts about
who to be,
what to do, where to be,
when to do it, how to see it,
and sometimes:
why should I care?
All these are fair and just,
but don't let your head bust.

The wise take a path and make two,
so you can have a clue
when choices number more than two.
Both are difficult enough to make you stew,
both have many forks of two.
So what do I advise you to do?
What would *you* advise *you* to do,
if you had eyes more than two?

Baltimore

If things had really changed since MLK's death,
there wouldn't be any riots.
Riots make tyrants question their violence,
'cause they can't get any sleep or rest.
This is a test, will you listen
when the bloody streets run and glisten?
When fires burn brighter in raging hearts
than the raging fires in melting tires,
you shall see the country tear apart
into a loving beauty to admire.
The bloods and crips
came together to end the violence,
just as raging pain turned into angry thrown bricks,
because pained heavy hearts had enough of suffering
        silence.
When racial opposites came together,
taunts and slurs occurred, one to escalate the other,
raging hatred in one, pain raging in the another,
toe to toe, an insult to the others racial brothers,
a flash of fist, makes both crowds pissed,
peace march forgotten, as dirt was thrown on a coffin.
We are currently on a cultural precipice, running into a
        wall,
and if things don't change, the dominoes will fall,
regardless of any condemnation
from anyone of any institution:
this is my premonition.

Perfectly Fractured

When love is mentioned,
Opinion upon opinion of this option or that option.
Boundaries and demands stacked high on such a small
        word,
Four letters strike such an ensnaring mystery.

You could trace your pen across ages unwritten,
And you'd find deep in your mind,
Boundless overwhelming satisfaction — bliss —
As love. And yet, you could paint it and miss its
        neverending turmoil.

You can't grasp it, collect it, save it, spend it.
You can't seek it, find it, curate it, kill it.
If it's not here, wait in the dark of your mind,
For the last one out of a Precious Box.

Hope is a transition into Love:
A desire for better bliss than now.
Love is wallowing in bliss with no mind —
Such a high has such a sharp fall.

And here, we wallow in its misery,
Turning a bright room into October gloom,
Might as well be a twisted sword in our gut,
Wrenching life with a scythe.

The bleeding stops, the wound scabs,
Gets reinfected, heals, scars, and hurts in the cold.
On and on and on and on.
A curse of a blessing, a strength and a weakness.

Love:
Perfectly fractured.
You never see the ending at the start,
You can't understand the start at the end.

Face Death

Face death
Like a one man army
Against ten thousand foes.
Scream your lungs into their valley
And watch their bonfires flicker.
Set traps uphill, spy at night,
Make them slip in the rain.
This is your ridge, a cliff on the other side,
Beat them back until your spine breaks
And your death rattles.

It's here, right here, that 'living' lives.
It's grief– that walks in after.
A sweeping November chill, dead leaves floating,
A creak in your bones: the pressure's changed.
January's wind suffocates your breath,
Wordless words form on your chapped lips,
Nothing said.
What's to say when your legs give way?
Bodies upon bodies, and for what!?
This ridge? This valley?
What a fucking travesty.
Might as well give up, give in,
Let the cold sink in. You're tired. You're broken.
That ridge looks so... freeing.
A twig snaps, a bloodied warrior charging...
Might as well... do nothing.

Imminent death is almost slow motion,
But you're frozen in place –
Lost in memories and futures untraced.
A chill, a gnash of teeth, an ungodly scream.
Death himself shudders. Mother's shut the blinds.
A demon,
smoking and smoldering steps out of you.
A smile spiked with a razor sharp scythe.
Swinging and slashing, blood spraying.
Terror in, terror out. Entrails hung from trees,

All the eye can see in the sunrise.
The demon catches a ride out in the shadows,
Disappeared but never out of sight.
There's a legion on the horizon.
On and on and on, it never stops:
Life's Onslaught.

Pack the tools, the tent, the food, the furs,
Time to keep it moving. Eat on the run,
Hunt the enemy in the flowering trees,
Trap them in the muddy waters,
Make them hungry in an apple orchard.
If death won't let you be,
be an annoyance to death.
Rock the boat, step on the elephant's tail,
Stir the pot until the kettle turns black.
River Styx ain't got nothing on
Relentless Revenge. And so you clog its rivers,
Body upon body, until...

You, the oarsman on the boat, gain a cloak and scythe.
So ready to escape the trappings,
You made yourself into the trapper.
The demon you released became a nightmare,
Told to drinkers in bars,
Children in bed,
Soldiers around a fire.
They all shake their head,
"What a shame, what a travesty...
To become what you hate."
A warning to all those who meet death on a date.

Sleight of Hand

In this sleight of hand,
Watch the falling sand;
A million thousand pieces of rock
Broken by a million thousand waves from below the
        dock.
As light as winter dust and as countless as the stars
And spread just as far.
Washed up by the waves,
Built up into strips of land that rarely behaves,
A single bird with a single seed,
A single tree was all that the land needed
To bring beings en masse.
It all happened so fast, sand into grass,
Land so grand it must be conquered by man.
But just because you will doesn't mean you can.
A hand gripped by a spear off to war–
Moves so quick, the bloody field was a dance floor.
In the end the messenger flew
To give the message to his crew,
Stewed leaders stew a cue for the battle,
A snake rears its hood and snaps its rattle.
Two fangs speared into a man with marks of power,
He fell and his followers cowered.
So fast he went down, never knowing
That from the wound, blood is flowing.
Seized by lack of purpose, he dies and so does the sword.
The army cut its cord without their future reward,
Got bored and built a city so bright and pretty,
That the gods nearly envied.
Whether by purpose or by accident,
God shook and so the earth went,
Shaking man into sand,
And sand into the sea, no longer so grand.

Dogs Without a Leash

Trying to mind my peace,
Trying to mind my anger,
Trying to mind my bliss,
Trying to mind my depression,
Like dogs let out without a leash.
Here boy! Here, sit, stay, lay,
But unwieldy they play, as rebel children with newfound
        freedom.
They roam, they fight, they play, they bruise, they lay.
I could scream, I could grow large,
I could beat the drums of war and let them break down
        doors,
I could let them rule me like madness to a madman,
I could ignore them and forever walk away,
To only have them nipping at my feet,
To only have them create madmen from madness,
To only have them burn down city upon city- more
        hellish than Gomorrah,
To only have them grow larger than me,
With a demon screeching, booming, and laughing to
        match.
I feel the trigger like a bundle of nerves to snap, just
        under the surface,
And decline,
Every. Single. Day.
So I sit, – I wait, with treats to match.
Carrots are bigger than sticks, so again, I wait,
And train, overandoverandover,
To the point that the word has no meaning,
And the meaning is felt through the offering.
Heads bow and sniff, nibble and swallow.
Spoonfuls of sugar to help the medicine down,
Because these dogs are just a few of my favorite things.
Rage feels as good as Bliss,
And so I know to feed one lean and the other fat.

Wordless

I am here,
I am there,
I am everywhere,
despite being rare.

If I opened my door
would you see into my core,
or would you not have the optics
to see through my neutral logic?

I'm placid- as a pond at the surface,
while, underneath, I'm raucous as the core of Earth's
          fortress,
but you miss it all, 'cause you ignored my internal circus:
so now, to you, I am wordless.

Sunset Upon Sunrise

Lesson upon ignorance,
Wave upon trough,
Sunset upon sunrise,
I followed foot by hand,
Food by mouth,
Sight by eyes,
Touch by nerves,
And I have nothing to show for it,
Because everything I've learned can't be easily shown.
Like the warped rocks curling in the waves,
I am the air knocking the sea.
Like the meteor that smacked and tilted the Earth,
I am the bend in the tree facing the Sun.
A hidden hand to what is known,
Revealing the effects that couldn't be seen
In an hour,
In a day,
In a year,
But by generations,
And eons.
Sit still and watch rock and shells become sand,
Sit still and watch the dirt and sand become bedrock,
And you'll see how History is the Story of Psychology.
Bend the mind and fold it at the creases,
Step by step and you'll build a paper crane,
Let the crane fly away only to let it return,
Unfold itself and rebecome a mind.
The building was nothing,
The return was risky,
All about how you suffer the lows,
All about the angle of incline,
All about seeing the plateau as it mounts,
All about planning the landing as you fall.
Two paths in a yellow wood,
        Dark or light,
           Red or blue,
               Good or evil,
                   Off or on,
                       Dead or alive?

                   So many
              Opposites duel,
          But little room
       Left for open
Third doors.
Third hallways will split into an entropy,
So many parallel universes I've spawned,
Uniformly different by differing actions,
Whether to not-act, yet always still acting.

Dad

you know that feeling when you

* Written 6 days after his passing and I couldn't get any
 further.

Hatching

3 am always brings you back to me
sticking like glue, my words — — —

my words are gone.
ALL I HAVE IS UNENDING RAGE.

I only stop punching walls
to avoid breaking my hand.
I only stop screaming wordless rage
to avoid the cops being called.
I only avoid walking out the open door,
down the street, and across the world–
to avoid finding out it didn't work.
I only avoid killing a man on 5th avenue
to avoid more pain.

So many actions,
I could live billions of lives,
but today and only today I am me.
I've been a lot of things that aren't me
for years.
And no one knows.
The hatching is painful,
the light is so GODDAMN FUCKING BRIGHT.

*Written about two weeks after his passing.

You Get Used to It

blood flows down steps,
into gutters and into streams,
smoke clogs the lungs;

a bitter bite in the eye.
the ringing never stops,
and neither does the heart.

you get used to it.
a dead body becomes a cadaver
and people become vultures;
a watch or a coat is better than gold.
shadows in the night slip past the sphinx,
and meet their end in flying lead.

you get used to it.

Dead and Remade

How much time have you spent on the dark side of the
        moon?
Enough to reside with the coldest of vibes?
Enough to find your way by the dimmest starlight?
If not, take a walk and forget your silver spoon.

Do not assume you can read these runes fluently,
For I've read the ancients in their crypts,
I read the verbose and sparse intuitively,
It ruined me, and in my ruins, I became richer than ritz.

Read my ribs, in - out, and right there is my clout.
Easy to forget. So let's leap, straight into the deep
Mind of all minds, cells and neurons, erase all doubt:
All knowledge of yourself is remembrance- so let it
        steep.

I could write and write, and my words would be lost,
I could stay silent and plan out the future as a seer,
and simply sneer, to see you as King Lear, - but at what
        cost?
No matter, death and loss abound no matter the cost, so
        release your fear.

Even so, nothing can prepare you for when your
        perspective changes,
A moment of deluded sobriety, raging deranged,
Like throwing red paint over stained glass, both dead
        and remade.
No longer the same, I walked with death, but not he with
        me, but my father- that day-

My dad: both dead and remade, stained glass skin,
        ragged breathing of tubes.
Ragged breathing of mine, sourced within the hell of my
        mind.
For knowing him "best of all", I knew him not at all; he
        embedded truth within a ruse.

A man to switch reasons just because you peeled his rind.

"Pay no mind to the man behind the curtain", a
          reiterated phrase.
"Thanks for telling me", and I dipped behind the screen.
And so I switched his red wire for green, the conman was
          conned, and so he raged.
A result I wanted, a result my nightmare dreamed.

"Be in service to others, son,"
A line repeated, but always to serve him,
In this, he wanted me to serve him- in thick and thin,
The moment that I stopped, I was usurping Attila the
          Hun.

Might as well be overthrowing Zeus, but I was too big to
          be eaten,
And now, I live with the pain of serving Gaia against
          Zeus.
Father-Son, both dead and remade, when will these
          memories fade?
Seasons after season, they grow, bloom, fall, and
          decompose.

Fly

fly.
oh fly, bird, fly.
open up those wings,
and let yourself fall.
when the time is right,
you'll know when.
let yourself fall.
let yourself go.
let your–"self" disappear.
let "y" drop off the word "your".
it is our time to fall
backwards off the edge.
eyes closed,
arms open.
breathing as if we were slumbering.
trusting in our ability
to fly.

Bella Ciao

Come for death,
Because it will soon come for you.
Wear flowers upon arriving,
Celebrate the ending.
No greater mystery than what lies before you,
All shall pass under its arch.

Odds and ends, babes without mothers,
Mothers without babes, fathers drunk to soon,
Soldiers spent as pawns,
Kings beheaded in the streets,
The elderly clutching their hearts in the garden,
Workers worked to death.

And still,
Bella ciao, bella ciao, bella ciao, ciao, ciao.
Spend and stoop your bones,
Hear the crack and creak as you age,
That sound is the music of your life,
Coupled with the heart's drums and strums,
Your lungs sustain the overture and chorus.

Sing loud, sing proud,
Oh, sing away the clouds!
Forget the beginning, know the end,
Bella ciao, bella ciao, bella ciao, ciao, ciao!
For there's a dream on the other side,
A mysterious dream, with tangerine skies.

Keep your heart still,
When they ask for more and more,
No matter the plead, no matter the scream,
These are your hands, your heart, your lungs.
Use them as you will. Spent, and it wont come back.
And still, my back is crooked, working this way and that.

So I hum,
Bella ciao, bella ciao, bella ciao, ciao, ciao.
Freedom in a bigger cage is still a cage.
So I sing,

Bella ciao, bella ciao, bella ciao, ciao, ciao!
My father, a felon, installed cameras in a jail,
And turned them the wrong way.

He still died a younger death than his jailer,
A younger death than his cellmate,
A younger death than his mother and son.
He worked long hours,
Partied all night,
Spent the last hours thinking, and slept not a wink.

He'd be singing, if he knew the words,
Bella ciao, bella ciao, bella ciao, ciao, ciao!
Lennon's "Working Class Hero" by any other name.
He, an ox, drove himself to the hospital.
Bella ciao, bella ciao, bella ciao, ciao, ciao!
He, a mule, fired for the same malady he cured.

Bella ciao, bella ciao, bella ciao, ciao, ciao!
And so I, the son, am left holding the reins,
His memories in my veins,
His wording lodged deep in my brain,
"Son, I challenge you,
should you choose to accept it..."

...Bella ciao, bella ciao, bella ciao, ciao, ciao.
Bella ciao, bella ciao, bella ciao, ciao, ciao...

His Words

"You'll see, when I die, you'll read my journal and curse
        me!
Damnit BRUCE! Fucking asshole!", a mocking smirk
        Filled with dimples.
"It appears I've hit the message, son. I just wanted to let
        you know,
We're having a spaghetti dinner tonight. Bring whoever,
        You know,
Whatever girl you have. Or just yourself. I miss you, son.
        Just...
Let me know. I love you, bye."
"Do you know what this is called, son? It measures the
        electricity in the wall."
"People are dying, son, it is our duty to pick up the
        slack."
"How do you think Ive been managing all this while?"
"I used to carry a membership card to give to people:
        'Bruce Burch is an asshole.'"
"I, for one, embrace our robot overlords."
"Pay attention, to the world around you son,
Look beyond everything physical,
Sometimes, the universe unites in a *serendipitous* way."
"Be in service to others, son."
"Hit the message,
Listen up, this is for the both of y'all.
Everything that I said about peace and love,
I meant every bit of it.
Now, I've made some decisions that no one likes.
You don't have to like all of my decisions,
Just like I'm not supposed to like all of yours.
But when you die, I hope it's the most vile,
Disgusting thing you've ever experienced.
That's what I hope for you,
Have a great rest of your day."
"You don't think I've tried that, son?
I wrote the book on Recovery.
They can't tell me nothing I don't already know."
"I relapsed and they gave me the cold shoulder.
Sons-of-bitches."
"I went to the World Service and presented changes to

them.
They couldn't have given less of a fuck. I'm mean, really
          and truly, son."
"You think your a step ahead of me but in fact,
I'm three steps ahead of you."
"Let go or be dragged, Mr. Burch."
"Don't let me downnnn, BRUCE!"
"If there's anything I've learned in my conning and
          thieving,
In and out of the underground...
Don't EVER....."
"Maybe, instead of dying of a heart attack,
I'll go postal."
"Get the fuck out of my way,
Or I'm gonna hit you."
"I want my headstone to read,
'HERE LIES
BRUCE BURCH,
A MAN WHOSE HEART
WAS SO BIG
THAT IT KILLED HIM.'
"No woman, no cry,
No, woman no cry..."
"I'm proud of you son, you and your sisters."
"What do you get when you cross an elephant and a
          rhino?
Elephrino!"

Oscillations

Oscillations position a point and a reiteration,
All things vibrating die with silence,
And this is where I try to keep my mindness,
Extreme ends tie the loop, twice an iteration.

If I composed a book with Laws such as these,
Would the reader see the Lost Ruins, overcome with
      trees,
Or shirk and scoff, baffled by grand words of Nothing?
Dig deep, and you'll watch Nothing from Something,

And it's Reverse.

Refusing to Steer

What a day,
Almost two years long.

A call that slowed time to a crawl.
A sight that burned into my retina worse than sunlight.

It broke into my house,
And kidnapped me.

Threw me in a dark cell,
And left me to rot.

I lost my pen,
I lost my vision.

I lost my heart,
I lost my mind.

I couldn't remember what fuel got me to alpha Centurai,
And back.

I lost the will to smell flowers
And soak up the sunshine.

Memory after memory flowed through me–
Crippling when driving in a rainstorm.

Death, I've met, I've seen it scattered around me,
But this? This was watching a fish drown in air.

A voice within me, so certain, so sure, a whisper in the
          gale,
"Just wait".

So the waves crashed again and again,
Screams and advice abound, but I did not take the wheel.

Steer here or there, the storm has us in a rhythm,

Steering too hard will move us out of space and time.

Cracks of sunlight through the lightening,
Had me envisioning.

Rain broke and restarted daily, monthly.
But the waves crested and troughed less and less.

The clouds broke at night, so I consulted the charts,
Remembering ancestors who got by with less.

And piece by piece, the puzzle reoriented itself.
My mind, a broken hourglass, was in reverse.

My vision restored, my pen found floating in the sea,
The sun dawned and I could smell my way to land.

Excited, oars broke the waves,
A large wake broke upon the docks.

Relief.
A whiff of dogwood.

What is Poetry?

What is poetry?
A ebb and flow of the dramatic;
a flash-bang of the theatric;
or the exact metric of inspiration— high in potency?

"The perfection of style is to be clear without being
          mean.
The clearest style is that which uses only current or
          proper words;
at the same time it is mean", Aristotle vividly dreamed.
In any case, whether nouns or verbs, poetry floats by the
          motion of birds.

Sappho sophized "Their heart grew cold/ they let their
          wings down",
and then on, the masses woke but forgot the dream,
          forgot the Crown of the Noun.
From there, Shakespeare asked "What's in a name?"
and Gambino circled the hamster wheel: "You don't
          need a name."

Neither does a poet need a name,
nor does a name need a title, nor does poetry have a
          purpose,
nor does a purpose speak anything, but how a human
          sings antonyms all the same,
for each drink different liquids but all raise the same
          chalice.

From the beginning of the first spoken utterance,
to the end of the most poetic prance,
it's all the same dance into the Dark Expanse,
it's all a Game of Chance; Circumstance; At First Glance;
          Perchance.

Though, Chance is caused by Actions within Universal
          Laws,
like Newton's cradle: from the actor, action is caused-

If you act-not, fame is not known,
if you act so, name is dirt or crown.

Either, flow at the ends like a corner that bends,
or slope like the circle that never ends.
If you speak, do not pretend,
if you're weak, do not lend.

For poetry will tie your tie tightly—
will load your shoulders heavily,
will add weight to your head, and will persistently
push you to think of things even more sightly.

Flowetry will br ea k

the flow, just to prove— poetry is the formation of
          stone,
some immense lines will extend and rhyme until the end
of time- as the ebb and flow of a lake,

while others are simply alone.

Poetry is nothing but a description of a verb;
the pen to the paper is but a description of the word;
the word only describes the poet, the poet barely
          describes a person;
the person is more than a name; the name gains fame,
          but it's just a diversion.

Many were only read when dead, for being dead,
their name spoke beyond sound, and spread through
          crowds by vocal cords,
for they spoke words and verbs heavier than lead,
and when, in the future, read— they were anointed and
          adorned.

What is poetry;
what is a word;
what is a verb;
what is philosophy?

A inscribed description deep in a vision.

5 Feet Under

I went into the deep, the dark, the dank black earth,
5 feet under, to rescue a man 1 foot from the edge.
He had done it for others,
Why couldn't I, for him?
Words upon words
Listed by creeks and rivers,
Listed under sleeping beds,
Listed by lit joints,
Listed by a son.
I lit the fire to remind him he was still alive-
A curl in the smoke told me he would never hear,
But would see it and nod at the valiant effort.
"Hats off to the boy who tried, but boy, I've done lived a
          thousand lives,
I've written the books on pain, retribution, redemption,
          and recidivism,
Don't you dare lecture me on The End."
So I listened, broke my back to listen,
Endlessly listening to the marked words of a dying man.
Page upon page cited,
Might as well have been a Dead Man's Dissertation.
I heard words I will never hear again,
I heard words I didn't want to hear,
I heard words... words repeated to me since birth.
And in all this, I saw a Man of Constant Sorrow, broken
          down by refusing to let go.
He never thought he'd make it to Heaven, "if it exists",
But you can bet- if not, he's feeding the Hounds of Hell.
A Rabble Rouser who knew the men and women still
          running rebellion in this city.
He divvied the undercovers from the restaurant workers
By the creases in their new blue jeans, crew cuts, and
          mirrored sunglasses.
They stop by his house in marked cars, just burning gas,
"Howdy officer", and away they'd go, zooming past the
          local smack house.
And this was the way it was:
"Son, wait ten years to tell this story...",

Nameless stories of conning and conniving ,
Might has well been Pirate the Bruce, from shingles to
lawn mowers and fuse boxes,
And then he'd stop to spare a man from the cold, with
his own tattered jacket.
"Here's some hot fresh food for you, stay warm,
          Godbless!"
He'd get home and throw caution to the wind, make
          jokes at God's expense,
Run out into the lawn: "Strike me down Lord!" with a
          toothless smirk,
And simply shrug at the crickets.
He'd have a good christian woman, ashamed– but
          besides herself, laughing.
What man alive would tempt the Fates and laugh like a
          child in a candy store?
What man alive would chase a man down, bat in hand,
          for a stolen flip phone,
All to give it away, the very next day?
What man alive shook hands with ________ _________,
all to end with a rap sheet, many times the Senator's?
"I'm Bruce Burch, Goddammit!"
It was here, among the centipedes and spiders, that he
          fought the Devil
Like one would fight a best friend, to only have only to
          have his adversary
Chuckling helplessly at: "If you shoot a mime, do you
          have to use a silencer?"
—
Chuckles turn to deep bellowed laughter, and the man
wrapped in smoke
Said, "You won today's battle, Bruce", and be gone.
Tales upon tales of a gunrunning, bat-wielding, son of a
          birth mother he never knew,
Dancing his way through life like a man who knew that
His son, "who knows me best of all", couldn't drag him
          back.
But still,
I burned fires as hot as sodium set ablaze,
And he'd shake his head with a glare and a smirk.
Until one day,
He bristled like a bear poked by a skinny knife,

Insulted by the cares I gave freely,
And so I rose to meet the bear like a bloodied bear
          hunter.
"Do it," said I.
A glare from the Fires from Hell met my own sulfurs.
The moment dragged into an Eternity, blood in my ears.
The Gates of Hell were wide open and silent...
"Bruce...don't", the gravely warning of woman nearly
          twice his age,
So he broke the deadly gaze and walked away,
          smoldering.
But me?
I wanted to drag him back, and give him the beating of a
          millenia,
The kind poets write about, plucking stories from
          History's Grapevine.
And there I was, 5 feet under, digging his hole deeper,
For three days- the battle raged, for each shovel load I
          tossed,
The hole I dug collapsed, under the weight of thousands
          of my memories.
And so I disappeared, never to be seen by his eyes again.
It was better for the both of us,
And now his ashes sit in a box on a shelf,
All that's left of a man I miss.
He considered me a son, and I considered him a brother.
What a twist of fate from a chubby baby in Richmond,
What a twist of fate from a closed adoption in the
          country,
What a twist of fate from the man who laughed while
          twisting the Fates.
And now, he's resting his legs in a boat,
Forever to light the journey for others,
Like he did countless times while alive,
Reminding them to laugh, and laughing with relief
          himself,
Asking:
"I just bought powdered water,
What do I add?"

The Fall

Love is a dangerous and precarious game to play.
It'll find your heart and grip it with an iron vice,
it'll corner you in the darkest of rooms,
it'll step on your chest with a weight of an elephant,
and yet, you'll always go back for more.
Because there is that chance, a slim chance,
that it'll materialize and manifest itself between
you and another. If that does happen- you will be happy
beyond belief, if all goes well, for an unknown amount of
          time.

And quite often, time ticks down until the end.
And if that happens –
if it does not last, you will be miserable.
You will be lost. You will be broken.
You will peer over the edge of a cliff,
and wonder what it's like to hit the ground. You will
          want to
hide in the darkest, deepest cavern, underneath your
          bedsheets
wishing for the day to end, and the morning to never
          come.

We take this risk because it was worth it. A relationship
          between
you and another lasted some time, and was euphoric,
          powerful, and
well meaning. But, the deepest of camaraderie, falls the
          hardest.
That's what we never want to see in love.

                              The fall.

Bull in the Labyrinth

I'm back,
I'm back,
I'm back.
Back among the light, the sun,
The flowers, the grass, the trees.
So simplistic to be here,
When I fought with the Bull in the Labyrinth,
When I took a sledgehammer to my brain,
When I dug my grave to hide from the world.
I crawled straight up, bare handed, nails bleeding
On the craggy rocks in the hole I fell in.
Tears of fearful rage soaking my face,
Teeth gnashing like a warrior facing death,
The muses might have been singing,
But I couldn't hear them,
The blood in my ears was overwhelming.
But I could hear my father's voice all day long,
Like the sound of china crashing,
"Number 1, you're just like me, accept it".
My mind was screaming in opposition,
Just to hear my own voice, full of a son's rebellion.
But a breath only lasts so long,
But a rebel only rebels so long,
Before everything around you crushes your breath,
Before the words "you're just like me", ring true.
And so, you could say, I jumped in,
And so, you could say, I fell in,
And so, you could say, I was pushed in.
All in one, and the same.
But still, I could see the stars,
I could see the sun,
I could feel the rain,
Dripping down the catacombs in the dark.
I felt my way, hands on the floors and walls,
Inch by inch, made mile by mile,
Until I knew the timing of water dripping before it dried.
Dead end after dead end, I mapped in the dark of my
        mind.
I was so weak I couldn't hold a pen,

But I persisted.
I was empty of all joy and passion,
But I persisted.
And so the Bull,
The Labyrinth's Master, found me listless, unafraid,
          gone.
"Finally, a fight worth having".
And he charged, full of bloodlust, full of rage,
And I dodged, more of a slump, this way and that way,
Remembering Tzu's thousands of tactics,
'Wear your enemy down on his own energy',
Remembering Laozi's thousands of metaphors,
'The use of a bowl depends on the part that is empty'.
Remembering one kernel, ancient beyond measure,
'The only enemy you have is yourself'.
And so I ducked and dodged with gusto,
I laughed and smiled,
I slapped the rippling sides of the bull as he roared past,
Taunting him, encouraging him,
Because he- is me.
I grabbed his horns and threw myself on top,
And rode as he bucked this way and that way,
Hearing and smelling me, but seeing not a thing.
He slowed, he slumped, he stopped.
"A boon for you, may you never return to this tomb.
Because if you do, I will end your life."
He knelt as a vassal does for a king, full of grace,
And I climbed down.
In a second, I knew my mistake,
He snarled and dug his hooves into the earth,
I turned and ran, full of fear for my life,
This and that way, avoiding dead ends and loops,
Around and around the labyrinth we went.
And up I charged through the hole I dug for myself,
Blooded fingers and gnashing teeth was my metronome.
"Number 1, you're just like me, accept it".
A scream to drown silence with anguish,
And up I scaled the deepest hole I've ever known.
I could smell the air, I could hear the crickets, I could feel
          the dew.
And so here I lie, among the Dead's headstones,
Alive and laughing.

The Pen and the Sword

I am the pen and the sword,
nothing can stop my gravitation towards
pens and swords from the House of Lords
that gather up hoards of gold within their wards.
In the sanctuary, one cannot ignore the needy,
in the penitentiary, one cannot ignore the vexed,
in the mortuary, one can see the greedy,
in the pleasantry, can you see their next hex?
The have-nots scrabble and squabble
like toddlers that waddle, watching idols and models,
but unknowing of the power and strength
that will forever take them on the longest length.
Humanity is variable, unpredictable, instinctual,
but always actual, practical, and tactical.
This is factual, survival is about revival
in the very face of your rival, simply primal.
In the quiet, the human is never silent,
in the riot, humanity is simply violent.
At the crossroads, who is the saint, who is the tyrant?
History writes the victors, who stood as giants.
Those that have many and those that have few
are not so far apart in the push through.
Arrogance in one from greatness,
arrogance in another from perseverance,
but it's all built from adherence to experiences.
So, in my deliverance,
do you see resilience or weariness?

Glass

Glass, oh breaking glass,
why are you on the floor,
underneath everyone's feet?
Soon there will be blood,
and screams of pain,
and you are to blame.
For weeks and weeks I will
find slivers of you lurking
around corners and dust mites,
even though I have swept the floor
a hundred times.
But,
it's ok,
I have calloused feet.

That Empty Bottle

You are sick.
I don't even want to think about you,
or even write about you, but here I am.
Now that your stuff is here I feel as if death
is knocking, knocking at my chamber door.
And if that's not enough I've just given you the
right to come into my sanctuary, my home. Since my
foot left your doorstep I've made sure you never
shadowed mine. I feel like I'm ten again, and Im
mopping up your tears, except, instead of tissues,
its boxes, and instead of tears, its items that
smell like you. How the mind never forgets a smell,
I'll never know. The smell of coffee, cigarettes,
and your sweat is in my nose and head like the
the smell of burnt hair. I've suffered much and coped
       less.
But I must confess, I do miss you. I miss being a child,
with you as my mother. For there is no woman, neither
       partner,
nor parent, that could replace a mother. There are things
that I miss, that I loved about our everyday encounter.
Your cold wet hair waking me up and ticking my face in
       the
early morning. The smell of your clothes. Your vibrant
green eyes. Your cackle of a laugh. The dimples in your
       cheeks.
The smell of your morning coffee. The high arched foot
       tap to
Irish Folk music.

But all of that is gone. Like that last drop of coffee. Like
the last cigarette in a pack. Like the ending note of a
       song.
Like that last dollar in your wallet, with no promise of a
       paycheck.
It's sickly, and lonely.
And now all I hear is the sound of an empty bottle
       breaking.

Over and over.

Gloves Off

You'd be hard pressed to write a new story,
you'd be a fool to think it hasn't been done before.
We've been circling the cycle, digging deeper in the
      mine's quarry
adding layers and wall supports to dig deeper for more
      and more.

The walls cant handle much more, the miners can't
      breathe anymore,
the canary is already dead, the braces and bolts tore,
and the ceiling is held by hands bloodied and soiled
that struggled and toiled all their life, and so now— so
      many eyes boil

with rage.
You'd think, with all this knowledge, that it'll be easy to
      turn a page?
"The age of information has no bliss", sing Old
      Songbirds deep in a Cage.
"No bliss leads to rage, which opens a cage", whispers
      the Cage to those who Aged.

Snarls smile all the while, silent with violence.
Humans are mirrors that reflect the laws of lovers and
      tyrants:
when gloves come off, skin and blood rub and mingle
      like singles;
the moment builds, explodes, and lingers with wet
      fingers.

"Wash, rinse, and repeat" goes the plot,
characters crawl, trot, and run for the dreams they
      bought,
as they move, they resell dreams as truth:
like bankers with bets on bets on bets, they'll crumble
      When they lose.

"Luckily, it's not the fall, it's the rise", say the wise.
Atlas' shrug rose and the sky started to fall.
Chunks hit the sea, hit the floor, the earth shook and
      waves rose so tall,
and as the waves approached, they washed away the
      foolish and the wise.

Two lost souls, swimming

Mid to late 90s,
A boy hid behind her skirt,
Flowers on cotton, blowing in the wind.
Traveling from state to state,
The car and road spoke their names,
From the hum of rubber
To the thrumb in between rumble strips.
"Just two lost souls swimming
In a fishbowl",
Swimming from oily motel parking lots
To buzzing lights in storage lots.
He remembers
Cattails swaying in a summer breeze,
Photographs clicking in a forest,
Eskimo kisses and wet hair in the morning,
Chicken casserole and robber movies at night.
Might as well been a flipbook,
Flipped all out of order now that he's older.

He remembers the smell of smoke in her clothes,
And the raisins in a marlboro pack,
He remembers her stomping heel arched
To the beat of music in time,
He remembers her slender fingers adorned with rings,
The worn pads in her clogs,
The warble in her laugh,
The memories unspoken in her tears,
The annoyance about a boy who asked "why" too many
        damn times,
The forgiveness in her embrace,
The God in her prostration for prayer,
And then came the madness in her eyes,
The illogic to her reason,
The shaky fear to her assuredness,
The chaos to her order.

Some things are better remembered often,
Some things are better long forgotten.

Take a Rest

So many reasons
To never take a break,
To never take a rest.
"If I can get there,
I can get here,
To get over there…"
And on and on,
Part of our animal brain–
Never to stop and think
Never to realign and reset,
And where are we now,
But up shit's creek without a paddle?

Keep it Moving

Restings too leisurely,
Time to keep it moving,
Up shit's creek without a paddle,
And you wanna stop moving?
Down there is a waterfall,
If you don't move soon,
So will you.

The Greater Me

Break the glass, grab the ax,
Swing asunder, debris flying,
Find liberation in the substance of me.
Crash, bang, crash, the Greater Me has surfaced.
Like the Angels of Old, the vision of Me
Enwraps those who see– with terror, with awe–
Including me.
As in me, so in You.
Birth the Grand You with as much terror as awe,
A balanced vision of the Ancients within us.

Fallen

I was 12 when I heard killing
words. I was shot dead when ears opened
to the verbs of a failed bird.

Mom,
did you fall
or jump? Did you run or dangle
your slippers
over
the building?
Did she, only 2, know enough to whimper?
Did you cry deeply
into the night, wondering if her leg would straighten?
Her calf that
    was no bigger than my hand,
      was
         curved.
           When you
     jumped-
     your ankle
       cracked,
   and your thin weight,
       turned her calf
         into a cast.

And my heart... br-

bro-

bro-ke, like a tsunami
deadly crashing on a small fishing village.
I sat on the shore in pure fear,
I neither shook,
nor cried,
and soon after – I felt nothing.

When you phoned months later, I was paralyzed –

but pressed the accepting green button.
Your voice rather shaky, full of fear and regret,
at 12, I knew it.
Back into the usual, I spoke
to comfort you,
but I needed your comfort.
I lost you, a woman who died in the mind, when the fall
didn't crush the body.
You had stopped eating,
only drowning in coffee and suffocating in nicotine.

The beauty
in disaster,
you were so very thin,
wrists half as thin as mine,
but your light bones were not so birdly hollow, so you

fell but did not kill her.

You, my underground foundation,
ruptured the cen
ter of my stanza.

Rage bent internally, pained my mind
into external death. I had to save-I had to
solve, I had to be the brace to your 2x4s.
But your mind poisoned
your pumping red blood, a virus that infected me
with

i n s a n i t y.

I cared for no one, a loss of me.
I sat in Dad's past and future van, named Odyssey.
"Son, you know it's not your fault."
and then ten years later, the same voice spoke:
"You know she probably jumped because you
left
her."

Father, oh Father, your birth mother taught you
that words are knives, so you, bleeding – cut me.
Further later, father you told me
that you played me –
spoke out what I wanted, and caused me
to leave Mom.
At 11, who is to say my memory is correct, that I,
and only I, walked away from Mom and her splintered
floor.
At 23, who could expect me to trust you, a smoking
        crackhead?
Ineffectively saving you,
I again broke; the 2x4s rotted.

So now,
back to basics,
I shovel out the silt,
bricking the foundation
with Ancient Diamonds of silt compacted,
sparkling further by Golden Mortar,
by poetic idioms that I read and wrote causing
the writing on the wall,
painted by me:
scriptures of a cathedral between my temples, around
the little boy on the beach, before more waves —
crash.

I look up, the wave crest foams
and curls, panic strikes
in me, I look and see that I am not ready-

surely the wave will flood and crash around my nest,
built of sticks and stones, that the crowd threw at me.
Between a rock and a hard place is the hardest place,
so I became the hardest Case that only I
could trace.

To live you must sacrifice, like the Ancients who cut
up martyrs and goats, I'll sacrifice myself
into my foundation to better me.
So,
lets see
how I see
when the sea
crashes over me.

The sound rushes, the wind chills
my soul,
my eyes tear from the focus
of staring,
my hair rips from my scalp,
the water smacks
my shelter like a hammer, the mortar
holding still, but the water pours in,
wiping off my writing on the wall,
the water
creeps
and
creeps.

Anxiety grips
me.
Will I live?

But I hold firm, and plug up the holes,
methodically separating the concepts of they and me,
that this building, built by those before me, does not
        hold me,
because in this disaster, I can swim.

And, in the midst
of disaster,
I laugh.

Nothing can hold me, nothing can stop me,
because previous histories do not apply to me.
I evolved and grew gills to swim inside me.
Only there, at the heat vents of me,
will I find the answers truest to Me.

The Earthen plates shift, and frictions curl and snap,
this mentality has caused the shaking earth,
which caused the cresting water,
which caused my evolution into ...

Poseidon.

Here I stand.

Slight

movements so slight
it was barely caught by light.
these thoughts create my rebellion
by refusing to believe in your medallions.
badges and patches award you respect,
but did you spite yourself out of neglect?
did you look down to find reasons to not be,
instead of chanting "i was blind but now 'I' see"?
did you seek the night instead of the day
because you had nothing to say?
or did you break it off before it died
to part off before someone lied?

On the Mend

Bent around the bend,
My mind's on the mend.
Memories altered
Like light through a prism.

He finds me– alone, or in a crowd,
And I hear his voice unblemished by time.
A caution, a joke, a kernel, a lesson.
"Don't waste time, son".

Friction

As the glacier flows, the middle is faster than the sides;
As the sun rotates, the middle twists faster than the top;
Ice pulls up rocks from the bottom, fertilizing the land
       for better crops;
Liquid magma magnetizes, twists, snaps, and roars like
       the tide.

Ice melts to water, dries and forms clouds;
Energy gives into heat and light, it's absence creating
       night;
Clouds drop, storm and thunder, creating a
       encompassing shroud;
Night rotates into day, drying up the dripping sound.

Without energy there is no friction –
No heat, no relation,
No light, no sight,
if there was no light would you have identified the dark
       as night?

Without the cold, light would burn all in sight,
Liquids would dry, and solids would melt,
The power of all or nothing,
Creates a balance between things relating.

Patronizing the Police

I've seen a thousand paths in a moment,
Walking up past McDonald's,
I never saw it- quite like this,
Predict a thousand, and miss just one.

"I don't know you! GO AWAY! This is MY safe space!"
"It's me, mom. Cayce."
"You're not Cayce. You might be *a* KC, but you're not
        CAYCE!"
"I cut my hair."
A pause, a head tilt. An expression, unreadable.
"Can I talk to you?"
"NO GO AWAY."
"Can I sit?"
"NO I DON'T KNOW YOU.
GO AWAY. I'M the CHIEF of POLICE.
I'LL HAVE YOU ARRESTED FOR PATRONIZING THE
        POLICE!"

A chuckle, "Good one, mom."
"I DON'T —"
"Good joke mom!"
A pause, a head tilt. An expression, unreadable.
"Patronizing the police. That's a good joke."
"....
Yea, well. What do you WANT?"'
"I have bad news, can I tell you?"
"NO! GO! AWAY!"
"Are you sure? I think you'd want to know."
"NO, I DONT–FINE. WHAT?"
"It's about your father."
"My fAtHeR?!"
"Your father has passed away."
"....
Your father has- passed- away." Mocking, unbelieving.
"Yes.–
I have some forms for you. He left some money for you."
"He left money....", a smirk, a gleam in the eye. Visable

20 feet away.
"Yea, it's not much…. I'll leave the forms here."
Papers to the ground, a stick as a weight heavier than
          lead.
"No! Dont! Go Aw–"
"Mom, I'll love you more than you'll ever know–" my
          words choked.
A pause, a head tilt. An expression, softened.
"Stay safe, and warm." A tent to her left, a tree to her
          back.
"I'll leave you be–", voice choked out beyond sound,
Eyes blurring with regret, grief, and helplessness as I
          turned.
My guide, a man aged 50, waited, 20 steps back.
"Thank you so– Much." A handshake to honor his gift.
"You say she yells at the kids?"
Far away, she yelled her dad's name, typed on the form.
"Yeah, sometimes. They don't want to involve the
          police."
"Is there any way I can speak to someone, to thank
          them?"
"Sure…."

13 years for one moment, and I've reviewed it nonstop
For two days. Might be a record skipping: "Patronizing
          the police!"
Might be the nail in my coffin, in another universe.
Might be the words to start me saving her– and failing.
Might be the words spoken to the Chief with a badge and
          lights.
No telling if that's the last time I hear her voice.
"You've done everything you can."
"Yea."
A voice in the back, guilt-tripping, nagging:

                    Not everything.

Caverns of the Earth

The earth could shake
and it wouldn't matter.
The deals, the guns, the fences
would all be gone.
The radio waves would be
the only living cultural artifact
left from our time.
Like ghosts in a ghost town,
our voices cast aloft,
forever.
Mountains buzzing with static and
twisted pieces of metal no longer
throwing voices into the unknown.
And Humans
so mighty and great,
crawl, once again,
down into the deep caverns of the Earth.

Survived By

Hard to know what to say
When endings are beginnings.
Hard to know what to think
When it happens all over again.

The sun rises just the same,
And today, it's too bright, too white,
Burning through my eyelids.
Even songbirds are nails to a chalkboard.

I want to laugh through it,
And so I repeat a Deadman's jokes,
But no one laughs– just a small smile.
So I lose track, forgetting how to cope.

I want to grow and heal,
But I keep repeating the words:
"I want to die" in anger, in sadness.
How simple to just— not, anymore.

A million images in my mind,
People who didn't know me,
Saying I brightened their hearts,
That I questioned their intentions,

That I was kind without measure,
That I was selfless, funny, smart,
Wise beyond my years,
And struggled against all odds.

And at the very end,
That I was survived by
People who knew me better than anyone,
People who knew my arrogant selfishness,

My pride, stupidity, naivety, laziness,
Meanness, my glum grim attitude,
My hopelessness, my hamster wheel.
The balance that I tried to keep,

The fears that circled the ceiling fan,
When the only sound was snores.
My dreams when I woke
On the warm side of the sun.

I can't leave them behind.
They showed up,
When others couldn't be found,
They said words,

When others were mute.
I can't leave them behind,
They fed me, clothed me, sheltered me,
Held me, scolded me, laughed with me.

But aren't I supposed to be alive for me?

Turning into Traffic

When jokes are made
About turning into traffic,
Turn the conversation about,
And let the wheels shake and scream.

Call it all out as useless, pointless,
For suicide has cause and reason:
"Keep doing what you're doing and ruin;
Head for the wall and don't brake or stall".

Cause and reason has been built up as a
Fortress with buttresses and walls,
With soldiers and cardinals,
With farmers and seed to sow.

"Stop and smell the flowers"
Is no empty adage.
Take time, or time will take you,
All this, I learned again and again.

I sat, too young to know,
In so much pain- enough pain to know.
I could see my life reflected in a knife,
And closed the drawer.

But the drawer... kept opening,
Of its own will, determined to remind me.
And I closed it, again and again.
Could've been a comedy, "Mr. Bean and the Drawer".

And so, at every turn, I learned to laugh.
At every turn, I learned to stop,
At every turn, I checked my route,
At every turn, I found bliss in the journey.

And so I say,
Where's your laughter?
Where's your emergency brake?
Where's your map, where's your peace?

A question I've posed to dozens,
Makes me feel all alone and distant.
Might as well be all alone on the moon,
Pointing at all the endless stars.

All our struggles are so small,
But we build them higher than China's Wall.
Hard to remember to look up in the rain,
Hard to remember to breathe and let go.

A question Ive posed to myself
Makes me feel like an idiot, when I forget.
Hard to be easy on myself in the deepest of trenches.
Hard to hold myself in the darkness of space.

So please remind me, when I forget.
So please, turn the bus 'round and snap the wheels,
So please, carry the torch when someone drops it.
So please, ask for fucking help– and take it.

Sky and the Water

One may start off with complaints,
But will complaints change the hell tainted pains?,
Will speaking truth loosen the changes?,
Or, will reviewing tighten the chains
By keeping us close to pain?
This is the change I hope to see:
A full reflection of the sky and the water,
The half to the other side, the sense and the nonsense.
Embracing the two, gives life in between,
But only if truth is seen.

Writer's Burn

It's hard to think when the writer's burn
hits you and you churn over the same thought worms.
Bottoms up, it burns so sharp, focus is lost,
bottoms down, eyes crystal and frost, a 3 dollar cost
buys a nice pen, a wall for writing,
if only there was better lighting, instead it's only
        lightening,
flashing and crashing, brief and bright, suddenly— no
        sight.
Memory continues to write, a muscle deep in flight.
No promise of a second flash, the writing slides
off the wall to the floor, and back again like the tide.
The ceiling-the sky is blank, covered with wooden
        planks
this pen is an ax on a swinging axis, cutting into the
        ranks
of mice and men; the writing is on the wall,
and now God stands tall, while you cry and bawl.
A balance finds you, peering over the edge of this ledge.
Don't get soggy in your own sludge, let go of the
        unworthy grudge.
Here I am, deep in this train of my brain,
here we go, shallow in this train of your pain.
God is no coddler, as we waddle knee deep, still in our
        seats,
is it now time to jump to our feet,
is it now time to set fire to our peat?

Again

Back again
Around again
The sun again
Here we go again.

It's a revolution to dance on my own grave, again.
Imagine me coming back, knowing that I never really
        left.
Contradictions abound, and in the center: focus is in
        view, but where are we going?
I can see so many futures, to only see the past repeating
        itself, again.

Back again
Around again
The sun again
Here we go again.

Red this rust,
Scatter the dust,
Rip open the guts,
Divine what you must.

Back again
Around again
The sun again
Here we go again.

You too, would dance, if you knew you're already dead.
It's already happened, so move there,
I'll move here, not much to fear, but fear, and its glare.
Such is the knowledge you come by when you've read the
        Dead in their Crypts.

Back again
Around again
The sun again
Here we go again.

Time Signature

With a swivel and a swirl
Pens write the world.
With a slash and dash
Lives end by the lash.

And on and on.
Might as well be the endless river,
Ebbs and flows; flows and grows,
To supply the ocean with drips to dry.

No fault to find in the endless.
Big bangs to heat deaths,
To asses in bars, and fucking in cars.
Might as well be a time signature uniting universes.

Air to Dew

something new will form from
        dew:
don't stir away from the truth, it will find you, and give
        you a clue.
within silence you will see, everything that came to
        be-
from land to sea, perched on a branch of an olive
        tree:
how did the silence come to be? before the before was it
        nothing?
it had to have been something, for anything to be now, a
        thing.
a blossom from something small to something
        immense—
things collecting and gathering from hither to
        thence,
examine the group structures, see them collecting to
        make anew
the mission seems impossible: changing from air to
        dew.

Run-On-Sentence

this is my message, speaking from the page
from beyond the ages: find your inner mage.
will you hear the ice creaking,
will you see the ice cracking,
will you step forth as it snaps?
sometimes, poetic verses are traps,
a looped thought, simply caught.
true verses are caught by a battled thought:
"roses are red, violets are blue
but do I truly love you?"
millions of thoughts swirl and speak,
the wisest moments, find two; the most opposites—
you think, you speak, your legs are weak—
the-mind-becomes-complex-a-
run-on-sentence-with-a-silent-esophagus.

Two in love

Two in love; one is lost.
One is lost because two was found,
three complicates the hearts state,
this or that, thee, three, or you and me?

To love we lean, because perfection
hasn't been created,
but by introspection we see our inner reflection,
then finally we participated.

Those that save are lost in the end,
those that were lost are then saved at the start,
creating further by opening the heart,
by more than two, participating to mend.

Quiet mouths breed loud minds;
loud mouths ignore the signs;
loud quills create the signs;
quiet pens disappear into time.

Broken hearts break hearts;
whole hearts heal hearts,
wholly broken and holy
hearts break off branches of holly for thee.

In the end, make a choice:
turn down the external noise and rejoice.

Universal

Universal concepts shake behind my face,
Will the muses confirm the ideas that I trace?
I heard the crack of the universe smashing
To create a new verse; instant creation

inside destruction. Those among the first
are the first to burst.
Those among the last only built from the previous.
Those that were remembered

stood the test of time and space.
Those that Understood – looked beyond the facade,
into the depths of contemplating God.
No man is an island, no matter his grace.

The more he sees, the more he claims;
The less he knows, the less he can change.
The more he reads, the more he gains;
The less he needs, the less he is bound to the page.

After growth plateaus, baby birds fly on their own.
After flight is learned, distance accumulates.
Stars are birthed in colorful clouds, then leave to roam
the dark ocean, leaving their life to fate.

Extra mass forms last, gravity weighs the situation
Then distorts the rotation, creating invisible friction,
That is only seen by measuring things seen
Against things unseen by which way they lean.

Eventually, the fire burns brighter
Consuming all the gods before it,
Burning higher and higher
Because oxygen was added to the pyre.

Some concepts wither and die, others gather and gather
No longer in its prime, god shakes up the design,
Its bright light suffers a dimming blight,

Explodes and erodes all in sight.

How did the dark come to be?
Before the before was it nothing?
Or even then, was it still something?
Nothing to something immense, by heat.

In the darkness things gather
Faster and faster,
Into things that matter
Just by being together.

Normal

To admit,
To you,
All I've learned, all I've been through,
All I've done, all I've became,
Wouldn't be right, wouldn't be prudent,
Wouldn't be sane, wouldn't be justice.
'Just us', a prerogative biased in position.
Do you, dear reader, know what it is
To lose your mind? Like it grew legs and ran,
Better go catch it, or run with it, like a
Sheepdog to sheep.
If you knew, would you work
In shelters, hospitals, rehabs, or congress–
To lift others, heal, reconnect, and guide?
Or,
Would you be tired,
Out of breath,
Lost and unfocused,
A stitch in your side?

A pity that those who know the issue best
Are often those that won't, or can't lead.
A pity to depend on advocates,
When you can barely speak.
A pity to envy
The hand
That feeds you.

Bend the line into a circle,
And it could be you,
Sitting on a bench,
Clenching the battle in your mind,
Deeper than the battle in your stomach.

No one wants to be ill.
But at some point, you forget
What it is
To be

Normal.

Elemental

Drink the Water,
breathe the Air,
walk the Earth,
burn your Fire.

The sparks lift up higher and higher,
to the clouds that drift and roll,
sparking thunder and lightening to admire
the Dark and Light, reverberation of cracks, booms, and
        rolls.

Everything I've writ was someone else's wit,
everything I've wrote was another's voice I spoke.
I don't mean to be a clone that drones,
but a dog digging for Bones.

Looking for:

A Skeleton to the Structure,
A Blueprint to the Bones,
A Map to the Way,
A Way to the Sky.

Up there you will forever wonder why,
questioning the sure,
questioning the unsure,
Answering from the Pure.

But Humans were not meant to Fly,
so after a fast inclined acceleration
flight falls slowly to run its wheels,
to fill up at a gas station,

cheap drinks and chips, then on your way,
on to a new day, chasing overtime pay.
Life on the ground is tangible, expandable,
and when each step is taken up, you step closer to the

Fractal.

Your Lungs Collapse

There ain't words when your father dies.
You sit, you stew, your lungs collapse,
your air is glue.
How to untie the ends and tell his story,
when he left 20 diverging tracks in the snowy woods?
How to uncap his character, when his eyes
held the fire of his words: "Do or die"?
People who've known him all his life would never
see the boy underneath.
People who've known him for five seconds
knew they'd need more than 5 hours.
A held contradiction in his cells,
like north and south on the same magnet;
and I, his first creation.
Any man could never his fill his shoes,
and yet, he wore bigger ones than his feet would allow.
Slipons eased his back,
cocaine eased his mind,
and I eased his heart and catapulted his mind.
"I challenge you, Son, *SHOULD YOU CHOOSE TO ACCEPT*,
famous last words when his lungs were drowning.
Famous last words when "I love you"
was only the last rites he needed.
I chanted Rigamortis long before his body was cold,
(He dead, Amen), and it was repulsive when he died.
Breathing tubes in his throat, fentanyl in his veins. —
But we showed up, the family he brought together,
to ease his pain, to see the man, the legend.
I could never conjure the man back up for you to see,
but you could bet, I'd remind you of him,
my words are his, my trailblazing are his wildfires,
but concentrated like the sun with a magnifying lens.
His love of the senses gave him to me,
his love of the senses lost him from me.
No doubt, his wound in me festers,
but I feel my heart ablaze with unrestrained instinct;
like a wolf, I know the trail to follow without thinking.

Open the Door

Nothing emotes better than weeping without sound,
Pain so deep, insides are wretched.
Let it all out, let it all hang out.
Few things worse than being a prisoner of your own
            mind.
Lawnmowers and laughter in the distance,
Might as well be 1000 miles away.
Clutch the fabric, feel its texture, identify its color;
Identify with the present.
Let it all subside, let it all melt away
Like ice cream in the summer.
Check the time,
Roll over, get up, and open the door...

Diplomacy

Some say "don't forget where you come from",
others say "leave and never go back",
in combining the two to understand whether to 'stand or
        run',
it depends on the day you get attacked.
An old schoolmate of mine
was attacked, bearing a brass knuckled line
on the tip of his nose, they stole his money,
they stole his dignity, all in a minute:50.
So today it's home he goes, "tryna stay out of trouble",
while I thought I was concerned about the latest
        economic bubble.
He gave me a moment to reconsider my internals,
so I gave back and laughed, strange to hear old verbals,
remembering the names
that tried to stop us laughing.
He had different memories than me,
cause I kept low and slack to the daily flack,
while he bucked to the daily bulls for a 3 day suspension
        fee,
while the other kid got the same and an ice pack.
He shrugged and said it was his juvie mentality,
meanwhile I've been bucking against west side apathy,
and unfortunately it's the diplomacy of our geography
that tilts us against our center of gravity.

Slide by Slide

Weep while you drive,
Dry up eyes while time is on your side,
This road, a time turner, memories- slide by slide.
Laughs and laughs of a dead man gone,
Lots of slaughter begat when he was gone.
Death leaves those living with dead leaves to burn.
And so I dance at the fire's feet.
And wait.
And wait.
And wait.
Imagine weeping because you finally feel alright.
A conundrum when your mind runs in cycles and spirals,
But it's alright.

Young and Foolish

dear sweet love,
sweet lover, sweety loving me- not another
we were meant to find it so simply,
we were meant to find it so easily,
we were meant to find love so steadily,
but we never saw it coming, never,
never saw the signs that tell each other
the other lover wants to seek another.
so we kept on through with kisses,
restaurant dinners, and midnight climaxed
assurances that two lovers were twisted
and contorted, so close— no distance was found.
but the truth is—
i got distant doing my work, you got tired of asking
i got desperate, you got bored
i got distracted, you got annoyed
i got it on, you moved on
i got guilty, you got distant
i got needy, you got it on
i got caught, you got snared,
how did we get there, as a pair?
a pit in my throat, my head in my hands,
all i can think is long lost kisses,
dinners, and long conversations into
the depths of the mind, even as we rock as one.
was it my fault? are you to blame?
i just know our love will never be the same.
we've tried and tried, but this air is stale,
i hate to do this but..
this ship is sinking, and i've got to go.
water is swirling at our feet and this is the ocean;
if we sink, its down to the depths we go.
"young and foolish" would title our stones,
together, but always alone.
this is why goodbye might be alright,
rather than get lost, lets step back and think
about where we need to go- and where we need to be,
maybe gain some perspective and see.
sincerely,
me.

Dreams

That sick feeling in the stomach plagues me.
when my hopes and dreams smash into the depressions
          people have accepted
—I become one of them.

I was always taught to dream and dream and dream,
and make it a reality.
Never to make reality my dream.

So here I sit. On the corner block of a college I never
          attended,
wondering what it is we're all pursuing?
Flash and shine? Perfection of an image? A dying social
          convention?

To Love

Growth is power curdled by evolution,
power is so many things, often confused by human
        beings:
power of love, power of hate, power of guns, power of
        flowers.
power of will, power of the still, power of the use of
        power,
and when to abstain from its use. All is so muddled by
        puddles of power.

Evolution is revolution of current practice,
All is practice, whether blinking or praxis,
Or acclimating to the seasons of a planet on a tilted axis,
Or perfecting the oldest maxims
To the next possible maximum.

Growth is revolutionary,
When the world's ends set to tear another asunder,
By a blunder of a simple verbal grumble.
War is de-evolutionary, but leaders and warriors
are caught in marks of territory, remarks so defamatory,
        or rewards of glory.

None matter, but the ego never sees how it can simply
        be,
But only all of its tedious injuries.
The ego is humanity's Achilles tendon,
So tender to injure over what it owns, but the reward was
        never "owned",
Never as a spoil of war to steal or trade, nor a reward at
        all.

Love is evolutionary to enact,
Because 'to love' is difficult to purely exact,
And even more tough to emerge from it fully intact.
A warrior's battle again and again, even when the head
        was clearly cut.
Few look before they step, and fall deep into bleeding
        hearts.

A bleeding heart had its arteries severed
And thus its art was clevered, to never ever, ever again.
I think the heart protests too much, by red blood cells
      dripping so much.
Love is no band aid, nor a hole to fill, nor a desperation
      to sooth,
But communication deep within to deep within, wherein
      no words win.

But love is not practiced perfect,
Because severed arteries bleed love. Bleating as sheep do,
"Love me!" the id-ego pleads, when only It- can solve
      its *own* need.

Empathetic Change

Try to change this and that,
then those and these,
will be against thee,
but some have your back.

What splits us into divisive divisions?
Perhaps it's our experiences, perceptions, emotions
that define our existence — from which persistence
is gleaned from the pages, and as we age, experience into
      ambivalence.

Change is slow, impatience breeds;
life is faster than before, so impatience furthers its
      seeds.
Some are empathetic only to those they easily align with,
and thus weaken the power of Emphatic Wit.

Some use the power of empathy
to further their own deeds, rather than to digging deep,
to change the shape of the earth and the sound of the air,
so all can see clear without bittered glare.

Empathy can unite us all,
or destroy us all,
by the degree that it is applied, when the Greater Self
      calls,
to voice the feelings in between society's walls.

We are the glue to the greater whole,
so, if we change, so does the world,
one finds one, another to another,
more turns to others, suddenly together.

Though too much empathy
turns off those who experience reality:
defined as harsh and mean, even cruel before high
      school.
How can we come together when each has different
      tools?

Empathy is strongest when felt closely,
apathy is strongest when felt distantly,
so to bring us to the same point,
we must be focused on the same pivoting joint.

If empathy is liberation, it must be founded on
narration and relation, to start up and go on,
to change everything for the goal that's long,
To foster benefit, keep our hearts, and sing our songs.

Pen the Paper Anyway

The days when I don't like people
Are the same days
That all the words I've written
Look like little piles of dog shit.

The days that I don't like people
Are the same days I feel hurt.
The days that I don't like people
Are the same days that I don't like myself.

How to turn the tide, when my own voice
Has two minds?
Lean into the waves
And pen the paper anyway.

Gold Gilding

i had to lose myself so i could delve
and find what it is to tie the world
into a circle, a spiral when its unfurled.
a phase you see when you look at your ways –
everyday it pays to write your book of night and day.
everything you see is beyond your reach,
unless you learn to forget the task, so you see the beach.
a builder forgetting bricks to see the building,
but if the brick is wet, it could never stand gold gilding.
in building bricks, pull out the sticks,
only a clean thought, no tricks, and look it fits.
but if a brick refuses to meld, give it back,
move to a new soil, and forget the gnats.

Instinct

Sometimes it's not so "do or die"
When survival instinct swings for you,
Like a robot with a brain,
Dodging left, swooping right.
You stand outside yourself,
Confused how you're still moving,
From night into day, and back again,
Around the sun again; you're still digging in.
Around you, leaves drop but it's out of place,
Like dreams and nightmares residing behind
Reality.
Snap out of it!, you try to shake yourself.
But the feeling persists,
Like before-the-rain during a drought.
And when it rains, it floods.

Revolution

Many speak of "God's Plan"
as if they know,
many speak of "God's plan"
as if they could ever know.
But what if— you could lift
a section of the curtain?
But what if— you could expose
the cotton of the stitch
long dissolved in the wound?
But what if you sought
what you saw,
would others see,
would others be free,
would you finally be — happy?
Or–
nothing would change,
nothing would look any different.
Though each climax exposes a new brick,
the new becomes an aging stagnating plateau,
until the new revolts and settles in–
yet again.

Silence

I might have a hundred thousand words on a thousand
        subjects,
But, at a certain point, words repeat themselves.
While...
Silence could be repeated a million times
And never lose its meaning.
Silence, waiting in the dark,
Placid as a lake in a cave,
Listening for the predator and the prey.
Whether to fight or to run,
Silence runs by instinct.
Follow it's route to the root,
And thoughts grow distant as
the pitter-pattering water down cave walls.
Your breathing echoes on the walls,
Your slowed heart- a war drum in the quiet.
March on.

Puppet Strings

What do I know?
Tall tales of myths and lies,
of my father— of who and how
he wooed by correctly timed lapeled ties and sighs.

Childish excitement bubbles between his chords
while I kept silent, to see my just future reward,
for being his conscience, with rightly spoken words,
though it was never enough, so I looked up to our late
      lord:

Grandfather, what shall I do?
What is the correct action to pursue?
Shall I throw him down the lue,
give him a deathly flu, or care for him- as I did for you?

If I stayed true to you, he'd be out the door,
if I stayed true to me, he'd be on the floor,
if I stayed true to him, father I would adore,
but in truth, I have to let him go, to endure.

Though when thought sits alone
rage seeks to burn out the pages,
burning though unconditional love, like magma melting
      stones,
filling with blood, my eyes see nothing but hell induced
      haze.

Play by play, what would father say,
"You're dead to me."
"Good, I imagined you dead weeks ago", those words I'd
      love to flay,
to hear sputters of an apology he'd blunder, each word a
      lie to me.

Another thought of what rage sought:
reluctantly I admit: — — I must let go,
for weeks, silently I fought

against the wish to spew colder than winter dew, so
        instead seeds I must sow.

Late summer must turn to autumn:
only loving the seeds will not grow them,
they must be tended to bloom,
and lovingly plucked from the tree, never too soon.

Winter hardens the aged growth,
bark protects against winter's bite,
snow melts into water in the slim daylight—
what doesn't kill you, feeds you the most.

So by spring, nothing will stop my bell ring
when I prepare to laugh my way to sing,
that you, father, will never strangle my being,
because my puppet strings aren't attached to anything,

but me.

Too Many Choices of Gray

The obsessions create a sound
That no one can hear.
I cite and recite the rites that keep sight,
And I swear, yet again, that it'll all be alright.
My gut is of stone when I know I'm right:
I'll drive home a sledgehammer
Straight through your scheduling planner.
Find this sound in the corner of my gut,
A feeling greater than luck.
Breathe deep within you and you'll find it stuck
You like a needle and thimble in a bumble.
Lumbering past the noises and sounds,
You'll find the Mystery,
The Great Reason Why,
The Great Universal Sigh,
A Passion to the Peace,
A Piece to the Passion.
But, can I keep the same passion
To reason with the Dark in the time of fray? —
I have my own insecurities,
Like "did I speak the right pleasantries?"
"Did I expose too many of my vulnerabilities?"
I could say, I have it all down,
But, I doubt all my capabilities–
Even when I have no reason to.
Pen the writer to real life,
And you'll find the same story:
A character awash in too many choices of gray.

Mind the Gap

"Mind the gap",
I fill the air with warning,
You might not be it,
So close and yet so far,
Might as well be a shooting star among the stars.

It's not for my lack of –
Anything.

Hard to criticize, hard to judge,
So here I stand, bending my ear to listen.

And just so, you, enraptured, don't hear:
"Doors closing..."
I grab your arm and pull you close,
Surprised, smiling, thankful, bashful,
And so, here we go again.

Just To—

Twenty paths in the snowy woods,
Lifting up my smiles all the while,
Mentally too focused on the end,
Remembering the bliss in the journey.

It's not all that easy to just– let it all go.
But that's where
I find my
Peace.

Going for a city wide walk, just to—.
Running the labyrinth of my mind,
Lifting blueprints from the angle of corners.
Just to—.

Connections

I don't really know you—
and yet
my heart is truly with you.
Fly, fly, fly! Spread your wings so wide
to grab the Earth in your claws. Bring us
towards the center, towards the beginning,
towards the end, towards the edge.

Every so often, my words fall out of use,
my pen daily grows dust by the inch,
and yet, when inspiration alights,
words fall out like water from the oceans.
The tidal fluctuations of my mind expose, align,
and redesign my rooted route
to find the shortest way out.

The way in is the only way out,
the way through is the only way around,
the way that's straightest has many curves,
the way that's most serious has many laughs,
the way that's most full is rather empty,
the way that's most grand has no opinion of itself,
the way that is this, is no way at all.

If you are confused, perhaps you haven't experienced
the madness inside the method,
but if you do understand, don't confuse
the madness as the method!
Methodologies are simply practice as praxis,
Study the movements, guess along the way,
Return to the charts when night turns into day.

When one follows the route to the root,
around and round they go, for circular patterns created
         and maintain this one verse-
When one sees the patterns as they are,
they no longer try this or try that— they do, they are,
         they be.
There is no sentence that starts with "I wish I could",
         for:

they do, or they do not, they can, or they cannot.
Becoming the un-becoming is a chartless path, laid
          down by the directionless.

There is no technique for finding the inner source of
          one's self,
only silence of mind and mouth allows the water from
          the ocean to trickle inland,
by the sun baking the water, forming vapor and drifting
          ashore, to drip drops.
The mind repeats patterns that were embossed on the
          brain, and yet,
cause this and that and one can wear many hats: there
          are reversals, returns,
and billions of turns, that emboss this and that under
          one's hat,
but the future is inaccessible, the past is gone, leaving
          only the current moment.

Who needs the current moment, when I can have
          everything tomorrow?
Who needs the current moment, when I lost everything
          yesterday?
Who needs the future and past, when *Now is all that I can
          truly see?*
Experience as my incorrect feet, perspective as my
          limited eyes,
understanding as my confined relation, existence as my
          constant creation,
I can know nothing but what I think I know—
but now, in this moment, doubt cannot supersede what I
          see: the Sun in Thee.

Sun Dappled

So easy, so easy, so easy.
It's so easy to forget the trees, birds, bees.
It's so easy to forget the sun, sky, moon.
It's so easy to forget the dirt, ground, earth.

And so I circle back around,
Reminding myself of everything I've forgotten:
Lost lore in tattered and stained leaflets,
The space of silence between each breath,

And then I forget again.
All to see the Sun again, gold glittering.
The storms had me left and right,
And now the Sun dapples pages I write.

Night into Day, and back, another rotation,
The Sun guides me, a lighthouse in the gale.

Falling back in line

Falling back in line
Is so out of practice.
I wander and wander on down the line,
Reinventing the wheel, just to be sure.

Falling back in love
With life, is so out of practice,
I wander and wander on down the heart,
Redrawing the flower, art falling out cart by cart.

Been here and there, as mom would say:
"Been there, done that", bitter suppositions of
Life learned lessons– instill deep. And so,
I look and see so much I don't want.

How to walk in sun, how to float with a bee,
How to let it go and let leaves flow?
There's so much I don't know.
But when the sun warms your skin

So much runs like ice cream under a summer sun.
Take it in, let the ice warm, feed the crops, and wait.
Lay in it, play in it, laugh in it.
Nothing compares when you know tomorrow

Will be even better. Nothing better than
Laughing so hard that you wheeze–
When you've wept so hard, you couldn't breathe.
Nothing worse than

Expecting the next shoe to drop, and whip all that sun
          away.
So wallow in it, when it dawns and sets, all over again.
Highs and lows have structure and form,
So invite the sun to arrive early and stay late,

But don't fault the sun for staying the same.

Work To Be Done

So much space between,
A laugh and a cry.
But you can feel the movement,
Under your chest, in your eyes.

Like the eye in a hurricane,
It gets worse before it gets better.
But out the end, the Sun glitters the
Devastation.

Grief, rage, elation, gratitude,
All out the door to the otherside.
But, push on.
There's work to be done.

Laugh

Nothing heals faster than laughter,
Laugh often, laugh long,
Laugh when it's funny, laugh when it's not.
Set aside worries and let it all hang out.
Take a long walk in the sun to find unknown paths,
Get lost and look for a sign, "You are HERE."
Listen for others and
Lead up the path to the next group.
And, again, laugh.

"Death inspires me like a dog inspires a rabbit."
Tyler Joseph

About the Author

Cayce Burch lives in Greensboro, NC. He enjoys photography, writing, and time with his friends and family.